AF399370

Robert
Ferguson

Love and Other Thoughts

novum pro

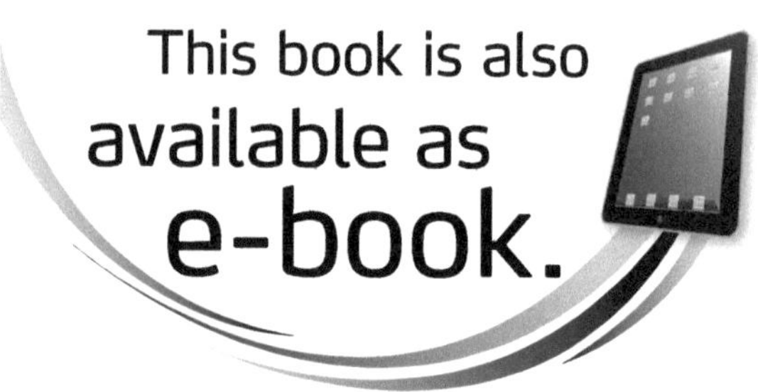

www.novum-publishing.co.uk

© 2023 novum publishing

ISBN 978-3-99131-907-8
Editing: Hugo Chandler, BA
Cover photos: Juliakarpyshyn17,
Bob Suir, Wirestock | Dreamstime.com
Cover design, layout & typesetting:
novum publishing

www.novum-publishing.co.uk

Contents

Control

Cooking, we control the changes we impose
On the structure and colour as well as the taste
Of grains and leaves and roots. We vary nature,
Under deep control.

Medicated, we control the atoms in our blood
By changing chemicals that none of us can see.
Add what is missing, eradicate what grows
That harms us.

Voices pass through wires high up in the air
And under the ground, under careful control.
Messages fly without wires from one to another.
Their transfers are controlled.

But love defies control, grows where it will,
Lifts and depresses everywhere it strikes.
Rules are irrelevant, and must always be,
For love is free.

On a wall in a Saxon church

Who were you? No, not you who is portrayed
But he who drew your face, pinned up the paper,
Pricked it through on plaster wet still
from the apprentice' trowel,
Joined up the piercings, painted your beloved face.

Or she. Was it a she who wielded pin and brush out of respect
As well as out of love, here in a holy place,
For the remembrance of her devotion and her charity?
Was she alive or dead?

What did her family say? What did they ask, or know?
Was your love secret, masked, hid from their fire?
Or was it shared with them? The face you left, sublime,
Suggests she had sufficient love for everyone.

As the sun sets and shadows grow
Her portrait glows, your colours fresh as when
You brought the pigment-rocks and ground them down
Here by the wall on which your gift was left.

So I must go, but you and she remain,
Always together, always witnessing
What each was to the other.
Always love.

Action this day

You were my first and only love, back then.
When, at the conference, I had had enough
Of being on my own, and now must test
Whether glasses and red hair convicted
Me to single status for the whole of life
I asked you out, and you, between two friends,
Tall, graceful, beautiful, a natural blonde
To my surprise and wonder, you said yes!

How grown-up I was then at just sixteen!
But everything to learn, and much to fail.
Perhaps, since all I knew was Shakespeare's wit,
Rather than grasped from rude experience,
I was too grown-up, formulaic, stiff,
Bought you those chocolates for the cinema,
Took you to tea one proper afternoon
In the lounge of the best local hotel
I could afford, with sandwiches and cakes,
And pressed too hard to see you every day,
So, with your lovely smile, you had to say,
"But I must wash my hair tonight," of course.

Did I frustrate and disappoint you? Was that why,
After nine months of kisses, guidance of
My hand occasionally to your breast
And rampant, unproductive, country lust
Which I dared bring to nothing, was that why
You dumped me? "There is someone else", you smiled,
And I, who should have fought, protested, said
Nothing. I let you go, shocked, shaken, stunned,
And took my medicine bravely, like a man.

I wonder, off and on, remembering you
So very clearly, as the years go by,
How very different life might well have been
If then I had been as mature as you.

Incomparata

When you said it was over, I resigned
Myself. No word would come to mind
To remonstrate, to ask why this must be,
To make you say what I could no-wise see.
I wanted, painfully, to speak my love.
You did not realise I had kept the glove
That you had always worn against the cold
Of winter walks, when I had been so bold
To take your hand, to steal a kiss or two.
Kisses have since been rare, far, far too few,
And none like yours. Hands I have held have felt
No more than paws. My heart will never melt
Again, as it did then, to see your face
Close to my own, raised to its proper place.

Stolen, one New Year

We met by chance. Adjacent seats. Both riled
With indignation at the speech before.
"Coffee?" I said without hope, but you smiled,
Agreed. I did not, could not, hope for more.
In common loneliness, talk came with ease
Until your hair swung as you turned your head
And showed the locket hanging in the crease
Of your blouse. "Sorry! What was that you said?"
Had it once hung there for a special man?
Was it still there for him? I never knew,
But, if so, for you, it held no ban
On pleasure, given, taken. Our time flew
That New Year's Eve. We danced. I stole a kiss.
Do you remember, too, as I do? Bliss!

Love across the counter

Eyes black, hair black, cascading down your back.
"How can I help?" you asked, your voice a purr
Of invitation, opening up a crack
Deep in my soul, anointing it with myrrh.
I was defeated from that moment on.
Brain-dead. Your captive. Anything you asked
Was freely yours. Any phenomenon!
A task of Hercules? But I had masked
This need, though I would lie down at the toes
Of your so elegant, so tiny shoes.
Immediately, memory lost its way,
Could not recall why I was there that day.
What brought me here? I stared into your eyes,
Unspoken lover under shopper's guise.

A student's lament

Where will I walk you, pretty maid, through courts
And cloisters, quadrangles and sunny rooms,
By river meadows, through the urban parks
Where racquets swing, balls fly, and girls in shorts
Sunbathe between the Council's beds of blooms?

You will not walk me further, sir. Your marks,
Much too inadequate, reduce your charm.
For I am moved by dreams beyond your reach,
And have no time for parties, punts and larks.
To reach the pinnacle I seek, I must be calm.

Be off, sir! This experience might teach
You something of a modern woman's place.
The world is different. Now, we do not screech
For power. We take it, with our brains and grace.

Wedding

White for purity, spirit, grace,
Innocence clear in hand and face,
Silk and satin, bows and lace.

    Pink for a girl, here happy, warm,
    Supportive, smiling, fragranced, calm,
    Will this bouquet fall to her palm?

        Blue for the ladies' hats, bags, shoes,
        (Not for gloves, which no one will use,
        Or ask any frump here present to produce.)

    Green for the bubbly's bottles. Corks
    Will fly free across knives and forks.
    Mark the end of the boring talks.

Gold cravats for father and groom,
For ushers and cousins, although soon
Laid aside in the heated room.

    "Ready to go?" Cans on the car.
    No need this evening to drive very far.
    Hotel, gymnasium and ice-white spa.

Socially withdrawn

You were a hole-in-corner person, never one to stand
Beyond th' immediate context you had reached
And shaped with satisfaction to your comfort.
Was it a lasting fear of something in your past,
That some Bad Fairy might one day appear
To resurrect, and prick you with the pin
Of shame?
          I tried to tell you nothing was that bad,
But, since you wouldn't ever speak your fear,
I had no means of reasoning you beyond it,
Knowing that I too must take the blame.

Was this the origin of what passed for our wedding?
Your excuse was that your father, near to death
(He lasted months after that dreadful day),
And mother (caring for him) could not come.
So no-one else? Bare side chapel, only four
Besides the priest, including you and I
And my almost-estranged parents, witnesses,
My mother, as always, playing the part
Of public figure in her hat and gloves.

Reception? Just we four for lunch that day
In a small hotel, steps across the town,
And then back "home", to where your parents waited.
In the sick-room, quiet in stress and fear.

No Best Man? Bridesmaids? Plural? What a joke.
I understood your bridal trim blue suit.
You had done this before, and failed,
As perhaps you saw it. And indeed
There had been enough fuss getting leave
To be married in church. I did not believe then
so didn't care either way; but it was crucial
For your Faith, and all your courage went
Into that interview with the Bishop.
I came too, but only to the hall outside his study,
Denied the giving of support you needed
And, then, I was most willing to provide.

No-one else, though, at the wedding,
At this most momentous moment? No.
Neither had anybody else we knew to ask,
Apparently, and so it went on, through our married life
Until your funeral. Then the church was packed
Some coming tens of miles, and hundreds some,
And staying for a wake, noisy with conversation,
A great success, socially, which we should have done
Long, long before.

The silent prize

After you had caught me with a seduction
Of which I had despaired,
And I had caught you with a conception
Which you feared, of which you could not speak
Until you passed out unconscious in the street
At night, walking home.

Thereafter you carried me on your back like a prize,
A husband, a not-husband. All I knew
Was your back for the next twenty-five years,
And I despaired again.
I had to test my unattractiveness, and found
It unfounded, learned more in three months
Of loyalty diverted to the pleasure
And the purpose of another
Than ever you had taught me.
Lies and excuses, but fulfilment for a while.
Then duty, standards and self-interest called
Back to the desert of two separate lives,
Two public faces.

But all this had happened
To you once before, and I, too weak,
Could not, despite temptation, cause it to recur
By leaving, as perhaps I should have done.

Now you have left me, and I, still alone,
Have space and time to look back and discover
What happened, why, and find the words
That neither of us spoke all through those years,
But should have done.

Tears for a beginning

When you were plucked from your mother
I was excluded.
Premature, I saw nothing of you
Until, through a hole in the side
Of your plastic crib,
Our faithful priest claimed you in baptism
With a borrowed teaspoon,
And I gave you all your names
Only one of which,
By insistence, you ever use.
My tears were not quieted
By the hug I hardly felt
From his weeping wife
Or the tiny white lawn square we shared.

Not friendless – were we?

Why would we be counted friendless in this social world?
We weren't, of course. We knew a multitude
Of people whom we greeted every day,
Sent cards at Christmas, even birthdays,
Sent letters to a few, just "keep in touch".
We thought them friends, but how did they think us?

We never hosted drinks or dinner, and attended
Only four gatherings of that sort
In all our married life.
I worked long, hard hours, with quite long commutes,
And we were never rich until retirement
When our health and strength prevented undue effort.

But others worked as long, got home as late,
And had a social life. Was it just habit?
Or a diminution of our confidence?
We spoke no more of it than of a multitude
Of other matters. That was how it showed.

The battered house

Come to my battered house and see
The glories well-concealed, but, me,
I know them, love them without fear.
I've lived with them for many, many a year.

The front door, useless now and locked,
Paint faded, leaning, might be mocked,
Its function only to offset
The upper window. Shutters fret

The evening sun with shadows dark,
The stain where rain has left its mark.
But, at the back, a welcome warm,
Where friends habitually swarm

To join with pleasure and with joy
To sup their fill, their sadness to destroy.

Gratitude

Fear gave me life
My senior surgeon's fear
Born of a life of sixty years
Of dodging blame under an alien rule.
A Westerner. A threat.
"We wait, he dies. We act,
It is the same
Perhaps."
He led his team
Into the theatre,
Slit me chin to groin,
Untangled, cut again
And sewed and sewed
And prayed as only recently he dared.
Thank God for fear
That makes a coward a hero everywhere.

Wakefulness

Sleep. Sleep. Oh, for the gift of sleep!
Darkness, darkness. Nothing to see through the eyes,
     But through the mind, memories of the heart,
     Memories in daylight long forgotten,
     Blotted out by action, blotted consciously,
But now returned, hovering, haunting, conscience-driven,
Driving back the very front of sleep.

And yet, is sleep a gift? When once asleep
Control of thought is passed from me to dreams
Which rise unsought and uninvited, aching, scarring,
     Comforts beyond hope of happening,
     Scenes beyond experience anywhere.
Wishes, or fears, or plans, or re-enactments
Dressed in new clothes, confusing.

     By morning, shall we remember them?
     On waking, shall we better understand
     Whatever meaning our unconscious mind
     Has offered up, during the darkling night?
Some, maybe. Will review improve our lot,
     And that of those around us? Sometimes, not.

Ending?

Shall we wander by the woodland in the dusk, my love, my love?
Shall we hear across the silence the last cooing of the dove?
Shall our footsteps stir the partridge nestling silent in the field?
Shall our passage start the sparrows who had thought that they were sealed
Safe for the night within the hedges as we strangers passed?
Will we be, of their neighbours, in that gloom the very last?

Shall we wander by the river in the afternoon, my love?
Shall swans float motionless, and, gently, in the trees above,
Shall we hear nature whisper as the breeze disturbs their leaves?
Shall coots call, drakes flap, raindrops drip from lonely boathouse eaves?
Shall our lips meet once more for a last kiss
Before we part for ever, swimming out to an abyss?

> Our wakings will be lonely, in the chilly morning light.
> Will you forget me, darling? Has our love been, oh, so slight?

Death, funeral, release

I cried out at your death, cried out aloud,
And held your hand as I had not for years.
They left me alone with what was left of you,
And I sat, numb, not knowing what I felt,
Empty now you had gone.

I sobbed at your funeral, sobbed,
I, who had not wept for years before,
No matter what befell us.
I read the "Seasons" passage you had picked
With deep, deep breaths, so near to tears,
The Vicar's hand on my shoulder for essential strength.

"Do not leave here," you'd said towards your end,
"I won't know where to find you,"
But I knew already that I must
Walk out into an always-beckoning world.
You did not like adventures as I do.
I have more lands to see, more tastes to savour,
Before I join you.

    And I am, and have.

Anger

At the end of our first meeting, you accused me of being angry,
And I was angry again because I didn't want to be accused.
I had been accused for decades with a silence more than that
Of the ice on a polar ocean. I wanted not accusation
But confirmation of my right to be angry after so many years
Of swallowing my anger under shows of moderation,
Shows, as I hoped, of mute consideration,
No longer even trying to explain why
I needed you to understand
I could not go on
Not mentioning
It.

When I had tried to tell her, ask her, quietly,
And she had said she would not, could not,
With a finality and a following silence
Impenetrable by any argument,
Any restatement in another form,
I soon did not
Know what
Else to say,
So didn't.

Frustration thus fuelled, fills a special tank
Like leaded petrol, full of noxious fumes
That eat corrosively eventually
Into the loyalty with which
I'd started and persisted
Far too long,
Weakens
The metal of
Its ageing
Frame
Until
It   breaks,

And I imposed on her the final hurt
Of my departure, acrimoniously
Resentful I should need to
Leave what I had hoped
Too long to shore up,
But could not.
Failure of us
Both.

I needed to know why and how we two,
Once fascinated with each other, sold
To each other's souls in admiration
Of the gifts we each had
That the other needed,
Complimentality
Personified,
Had failed.

And all I got was fire-eyed accusation. I suppose
Maybe you did feel what I was describing, but
You couldn't, wouldn't, try to see my side.

Over the threshold

I went out in the morning and couldn't dance or sing
What would the neighbours see or say?
Whatever could I bring
To the world which bears down on so many people?
I hid myself away
Behind the tasks I had to do, the busyness of the day
I did my duty, kept my word, fulfilled my promises
It passed the time but still
The longings buried deep inside
My nature, what and who I am, remained
Unsaid, unshown, my secrets
Unexpressed but gnawing
Too late now
Or is it? Why should they care
Or even notice?
So I raised my voice, my arms, my heels
Offered myself where I might be accepted
And was

Pot'mus

He isn't noble, ethnic or expensive
I got him from a common catalogue
Reconstituted stone in someone's garage
Mould made for a hobby
Copies made for profit
But you loved him for the glorious gurgling laughter
You heard him always utter when your eye
Caught his as he sat on his shadowy side-shelf
Mouth always open in a happy guffaw
Which you always echoed.

Now you have gone, I keep him in that same place
And he never fails to make me guffaw too.

Through the ceiling
(Danny, 1988)

Look up above you.
What colour is your ceiling?
So was our team until,
Cheerfully, confidently,
He applied.
Selection was by the colleagues
With whom he'd work
So they were careful
Of the quality we recruited.

He was good.
Wrote well,
Spoke well,
Smiled his great wide smile,
Broke through the ceiling
Was a huge success.
Our contribution.

A gentleman caller

Rooster in the farmyard,
       Cowdog dozing.
Between the barns, green pastures,
       Bird-filled hawthorn hedges. Friesian cows
Chew moodily as the gentleman
Leaves the road and struggles up the track
To the farmhouse back door,
Jute sack on his shoulder.
"Glass of water, Missus?" "And a sandwich?"
She says. They've met before
And know he'll soon be on his way,
Unhurried, to his next port of call.

Two for joy

Good morning, Messrs Magpie! You've been out late
From last night's formal dinner. You're still smart,
Though, in your well-pressed black-and-white.
Was the mayor there, or the local M.P.?
Did you go on to a club, or a casino, afterwards?
Whatever, here you are in the dawn light,
Floating with dignity over the public park,
Gliding between the trees until you see
A leaf-strewn clearing, and you drop to land
With a brief run to settle yourselves,
Beaks down, throwing aside the leaves
To expose the tiny seeds for breakfast,
Or strut to flap up onto the rubbish bin,
Throw out the card and plastic, and then search
For sausages and chips. Then off again,
Flashing your black-and-white for someone else.
But I have seen you both together this morning,
And thank you for bringing blessings on my day.

Spirits of the Spring

My garden is edged by evergreen bushes
Ageing and slightly overgrown, as I am
Last Spring, they were settled by two families of blackbirds
Who brought up two youngsters each, in the hot summer sun
And fled the approaching chill of winter
Leaving me deserted

But in the increasing mildness
Two males have returned to assess what is left
Of their last-year's nests, and perhaps repair
The depredations of passing time
As I might revisit the ruins of past places
Replace tiles, unblock gutters
Preparing for females, who may also remember
Loyally, the happiness of former locations
Where fledglings were safe and well-fed

Or are they simply the spirits of past years
Whose function is heralding a new year's progression
Of time ever rolling, unstoppable, continuous
The same as it has been, but different again

On the river

There they go, puffing their chests and flashing their oars in
the sun.
Ones and twos and fours and eights, their so-called boats so slim
As to be invisible. You'd think they were training and
straining
To join a crew for a modern Battle of Lepanto,
                                 all effort and sweat and pride.

Not me. My tubby skiff suits me. Gently we paddle, when I
feel like it,
Along the near-side bank, close to the reeds and willows
Dripping into still water, and considerately past the anglers
And their lines and floats, poking into grottos built of leaves
Arched over the water. Slowly. What's the point of dashing
Over the silver mirror of the water? To get where?
And having got there, where then except back?
No, I'm a mole-and-water-rat man. I dawdle,
'Cos there's nothing, absolutely nothing, as pleasant
As messing about in a boat.

Dog, running

Locked in the house all night, alone, downstairs.
All the family has long retired,
Or, adept at the threat of claws on doors
And walls, maybe in warmth and comfort
On a bed.
                    But now it's morning!
                    Child ready for school,
                    Leash raised –
Do they all really think that I don't know
It's time for me to walk them? Exercise
Will build their bodies up and do them GOOD!
Come on! Come on! Yes, quickly,
Open the door, so I can – oooh, aaah, oh,
That's better – so I can concentrate again.
And here's the park. Hurrah!
Leash off, my liberty, away I go,
Running! My legs a whirr.
            And there's that tree where all my friends and I
            Pause in respect to sniff and mark our turn,
            Then off again at the run to Council beds
            Of yellow pansies, row and row on row.
But what's this? Mistress' call? Oooh yes, it is
That foul-whoofed terrier who every day
Tears round and terrorises decent dogs.
Safety lies beside my mistress' legs for just a while.
Then off again, until my breath has gone
And, sated, we can walk sedately home.

Hard times

"This is the bit I still like," he mumbled,
Farmer-like, "The bit that's still the same.
Bringing them in, and bringing them back again,
Following their black-and-white backsides down the lane.
I've done it all my life, see?
Not like the milking now. Used to do them all by hand,
All seventy of them, in my old dad's time.
Took three or four hours. Now the suckers go on them
Automatic, each one in her place,
And come off when they've finished.
They neither notice nor care,
Just chew their feed, and stand there.
Often, hand-milking, they'd play up,
And then you'd have to mind your toes, or else!
Big beasts they be when they've a mind to use their weight.
An' all this computer mither, and reports, and vets' checks.
Our Betty has to do that, now she's out of school.
I can't. And the price goes down and down.

A few round here gave up last winter.
Me, I can't. Couldn't be without the beasts,
And the dog, and the land. Knowing it's all mine.
But make a living? Naw! But then, who knows,
Maybe 'twill turn up again next year.
I can hang on 'till then, I do suppose."

Silent sounds

The rocker creaked as Auntie stirred.
Dozing, she'd call it; sound asleep.
Even when Cleo dropped lightly
Onto her lap from the table
Without a sound, and stretched out,
Turning her eyes to Auntie's face,
Showing her teeth in a silent
Miaow of greeting, unacknowledged
But for the gentle, quivering,
Hand-shaking, shoe-slipping whistle
Of the hint of a slight, quiet snore.

Calm in the Sun
(Garden of the Royal Palace, Seville, Andalucía)

Long hedges. Long, long hedges
>High enough to cast shadow
>Even in the almost-overhead sun
>On the paths beside the long, long fish-tanks
>In the depths of which
>>Weed shadows wriggling red-gold arrows
>Lazily waving their tail-fins
>With all the time in the world.
>Caliphs found calm here
>From the stressful demands of governing
>From the need to seem strong in their courtiers' eyes
>From the heat of the small-windowed palace
>From the reminders of scripted tiles.
>And, strolling as never possible
>In the rushing life of business and family,
>So do I.

Garanat, the pomegranate city

A thousand years ago, no woman's face was seen
Uncovered in these same streets
And men in long robes swished their way
Squeezing themselves between white walls
Over the narrow cobbles, greeting their friends
With handshakes and a blessing prayer
As they touched mind, mouth, heart in thanksgiving.
Their donkey carts climbed these steep slopes occasionally
Labouring to bring food from the *vega* fields
Or taking fruit from the shady *carmen* gardens
To family and friends.

Punctuated by the spires and towers of baroque churches
Built into the minarets of Moslem mosques,
Wide, sun-filled *plazas*, tree-lined *avenidas*,
Suddenly surprise the wanderer who slips
Through an ancient shaded colonnade
To rest for a moment, even for an hour,
With coffee, tea as they used to do, or glass of wine.
A thousand years ago, life moved more slowly
Passing by the same steps we follow, even today.

Now buses, cars, scooters, trucks all rush
Through gaps impossible, centimetres spare.
Tourists wander, stop, get lost, consult their sat-maps.
Everyone, young and old, talk on their 'phones
Gesticulating constantly to unseen friends.
And women wear their bodies as works of art
In the briefest fashions that they dare.

Hammam
(The Arab Baths)

The candles in their antique fretted lamps
On and around small fountains
Add little to the light from ceiling stars.
The gloom is dense, heavy, windowless of course,
For we are here to feel and not to see.
Floors are tiled smooth for wet bare feet
Around the step-down, hot, warm, cold, dark baths
In which we float, buoyed by the water brought
From the sacred mountain up above the town
By aqueducts constructed a thousand years ago.
Massage rooms, silent, are alcoved
Each with a bed, a masseur, peaceful, still,
Except for the caring, healing, strengthening hands
At work with scrubs and oils to wipe away
The stress and tension of a modern life
Preparing each body for the coming day.

Left in a black binbag

Screwed up, discarded, bundled to one side
A scumbled sheet in blackball wax with gaps
As though some words displeased the ache-kneed artist
Stretching tired calves and toes, reviewing time

Stretching tired calves and toes, reviewing time
Spent in the saddle under tropic sun
Hoping that peers' approval will result
In a brass plate recording how he lived
And died in service far away, unknown.

The digital forty-niners

He was here early, pegged his claim out tight,
Convinced beyond all doubt that it contained
His fortune. Dug and continued digging,
Drilled, charged and fired, shovelled the gangue away
And dug again without success until
Desire and muscle died. Gave up the claim
As hopeless, walked away, and never heard
That Greasy Jim struck ore only a foot below
Where he had stopped. Jim sold the claim
For millions, which he promptly drank away.

Two pools of blood

2 April 2018, Tottenham and Hackney

Two more pools of blood have disappeared,
Swashed out with a bucket of sudsy water,
Mopped away, as Edna mops her kitchen floor
Now and then, only more promptly, as soon as the Filth had gone.
And the chalk outline.

"Do it!" It's no kindness to leave that reminder
Of kids cut down, children we watched grow up,
To make their Mums start crying all over again,
Or go the long way round when they go to the shop,
To avoid them.

"We'll grieve at the funeral, and after
In the pub. Do it! Wash away our shame
At the memory of cardinal sin forgotten.
'Thou shalt not kill!' says the Good Book."
But they did.

    The whole street, the whole district, knows
    Who did it, knows who rented the gun, who sold the knife,
    Who went out that night to kill those kids.
    For what? For pride, for power, to be the Big Man
    No-one dared oppose?

    Everyone knows, but not a soul will tell.
    Not just from fear for themselves,
    But for their own kids, their Bro's, their boyfriends
    Still running or rivalling those who did these deeds
    That bloody night.

Why do they do it? Why will they still join?
What else is there for them? "Ain't no jobs,
An' if we do, we have to work. Some bastid bosses us,
Gives no respec'. This is the easiest way to pass the time."

"That's all life is for us. We're given time
And nothing else. We're left to fill it. Boring!
Joining gives us somewhere safe to go,
Heroes to admire, just as long as we all do the same,
Watch the same, listen to the same, say we believe the same,
Carry the same, fight the same, hate the same,
Kill to protect the same, and mark our passing
In more pools of blood.

Sulawesi tsunami, September 2018

Here we are, perched on a circling orb
just the right distance from our central star
the only one sustaining life perhaps
so privileged, chosen, mostly safe, secure
until we are reminded that this life
is delicate.

When the Earth moves, and oceans rear
in anger, life in all its glory
is wiped out.
Now as not before we know the what and how
this happens, but we do not know
the why.

Are we the greatest power
or is there something greater we can't see
with a purpose we dare not consider,
for whom our self-importance is a sham?

Bahnhof, Köln

When the world's harshness appals me,
When freedom is threatened and barriers built
Between peoples who otherwise reached out their arms
To bid welcome, their hands warm to greet,
I remember the kindness they gave me, at night,
When the station, deserted of trains, simply echoed
To the unison footsteps of uniform boots
As they checked I was all right, no threat to their city,
And left me to sleep on their welcoming bench.

A toehold in Freedom

It had been a clear night, almost calm.
What little wind there was chilled our left cheeks
As we followed the star pointed out by our despatcher.

"That's North," he'd said. "That's England."
We could see lights from where we set off.
We'd seen them sometimes even from Calais
And dreamed. One day, we'd hoped, one day…

"Sit still, go slowly and you'll be safe," he'd said,
But these were people who'd never seen the sea,
Nor even read about it. Lights, white, red and green,
Showed far above us in the Dover Straights,
Repeatedly. Sometimes we heard the throbbing
Like a huge heart in their great steel body,

And knew to let them pass, so their displacement
Would not swamp us. Soon it would be day.
We might be seen and picked up, maybe,
And, praise God, we were.

Arrested, landed, we were all relieved
And made our applications for asylum
To officers, firm and duteous, but more gentle
Than those we'd known at home.

"Family in England?" they'd asked.
We all said "Yes".
"Where?" they'd asked next.
"Our Uncle Ahmed in Folkestone",
We replied as we'd been told to do.

Soon we were among our own people once again.
They'd find us jobs, a room, or send us on.
It wouldn't be easy, but, despite our fears,
At last we had a toehold. We were safe!

As it was

(for Sarah)

Earth Mother, soft and all-embracing
Healer, herbalist and carer
For daughters who might follow in her footsteps
Into age-old mysteries of Creation
Picking, boiling, learning, consulting, writing,
Filtering, corking, bottling, taking, giving,
Spreading helpful good in ancient ways.

High on the mountain

High on the mountain
        there is nothing.
Nothing for you to see, anyway.
Above the street - there is only one –
and the tip-heaps along the valley side,
all grassed over now
        except where they've slipped and scarred
        in the winter wet.
There is only the spiked, coarse grass
That the sheep eat
        for want of better,
Gorse they'll eat when they have to,
        prickles and all,
Scree, grey, treacherous,
        on its way to fill in the cwm
        in a few thousand years,
The outcrop with the low, shallow adit
        intended to yield silver
        a few thousand years ago,
A few ewes, a ram,

And the wind.
Ever the bitter wind
cutting through you.

        I told you.
        Nothing.
Nothing for you to see, anyway,
Till the Little People come
        as the darkness gathers,
        to dance in their rings
        and teach the lambs to gambol,
and nip wool from the sheep for their spinning,
        And tell their spells.

A wasted weekend

They dropped me at a tiny rural station.
Strangers. Uncaring. "You'll soon get a train.
Remember to change at New Street, Birmingham."
I had known no-one. Why was I invited?
Enthusiastic hostess welcomed me,
And disappeared. Saw no-one again
Nor husband? father? partner? all weekend.

No ticket office, buffet, bench or shade.
After two hours, a sun-baked porter walked
Grudgingly up the sloping platform-end,
"How long have you been here?" I couldn't answer.
"B'r'm trains go from over there," he offered.
I looked. No footbridge. "Cross the line", he said.

Visible in the distance, silently,
A silver worm caught the sun around the bend,
Drew in, consumed me and my battered suitcase.
Gradually, we left the countryside, the cows,
The horses, space, the trees, the loneliness.
Suburbia stretched out its welcome arms
To claim me back, a city boy come home.

What, again?

She's done it again! Jumped in front.
And I was here first! Or fourth.
At least, before her! And, yes, in fact, I do mind,
Despite her smile, her simpering, insincere, artificial smile!
And she trod on that dog's paw in her rush to get to the
counter!

But, if it means so much to her, why should I care
At the thoughtless unfairness of her pushing in?
I can ignore it. I might even forgive her one day.
Who knows, in time, I might go so far as to forget.
I have nowhere else to be at just this moment.

"Who does she think she is?" I hear them mumble
From the back of the queue. I heard it last week too
When again she did it, and took the very last slice
Of my favourite cake.

South Yorkshire

The winding gear, now silent, stands
Each end of narrow, grimy streets
Up which square men in black caps cough
Their way to shops for fags and news,
And sweeties for occasional kids
Sent by their mothers to make sure
That Grandpa's still alive, and knows
They love him, though it's seldom said.

A mile away, on the next ridge,
Another winding gear still stands,
And two miles South, another,
But no-one has a use for them.
Cows graze beneath them. Buzzards perch,
But all is quiet in this land.

Regina
A fragment lost from the folio and recently restored

The English Court. Enter Queen, attended.

Qu.   What? Can this noble land no longer breed
        Men of clear thought and foresight? How's it come
        That only braggart fools stride on Our stage,
        Liars and empty optimists, without
        Capacity to see the needs of those
        Who might oppose them? Do they but believe
        That twenty miles of water will reduce
        Our neighbours' minds to those of peasant folk,
        Untutored in the diplomatic arts?
        They are but bullies, arrogance itself.
        He and his ally Somerset stood there
        Before us, giving us the lie, smug smiles
        Upon their faces, thinking me a fool
        Who could not challenge their transparency.

Fie on them, fie, and on my forefathers
Who gave away the power of Crown to them.
Will they divide the country? Is it war?
What say you, Cambridge? Can there be a plan
To overcome them, e'en at this late hour?
Send out your spies, discover what you can,
For We will not allow their strategies
To wreck Our realm and throw Our people down
Into dire poverty and joblessness.

Exit Queen, angry but determined.

The bell

The four-ton bell
Came loose and fell
Descending as if it were under a spell.

The clocktower threw
The same shadow. Just a few
Failed to gather for what would ensue.

The mayor was called
But stalled.
He was totally appalled!

In the crowd
A whisper passed, as if a shroud
Were lifted. All were cowed.

Landing, the bell exposed
The Town Hall cellar. Pipework was disclosed
And broken. Water hosed

And rose in the resulting cavern.
Floors collapsed. The mayor looked stern.
Councillors' faces stiffened with concern.

"Never mind," a cheerful voice declared,
"We'll build a new Town Hall," but anger flared.
"We don't want change. We want the old repaired."

Surveys showed this was not possible.
After months of wrangling and hassle,
They built the new just like the old, but cyclical

So it would fall down every fifty years.

Waterwheel

I was first hung here a thousand years ago,
Made of good English oak
And mounted on oak posts and oaken spindle,
And the stream that rushed past me,
                              pushed me, then
Was the same stream running past me here today.
        There it is below, but take great care!
Don't go too near, and slip.
        You won't come out alive,
For I can't stop myself, once I'm unbraked.
I've too much power, you see – as well as hear.

What was I for, you ask? At first, for flour.
A miller built me, owned me. All around just then
Was forest. Not just woodland,
                open, sun and shadow striped,
But deep, thick forest, so the great noble Duke
Who owned this land, and taxed its work,
Might peradventure neither see nor hear
My turning; and he didn't, until envy told my tale.
The miller hanged, then I was left for dead.

Until the trees were cleared, and wool and linen cloth
Required my services. Why, do you ask? For fulling.
Bless your life, to not have heard of that!
But maybe you don't do it any more,
Or not in mills the size of this, I'd say,
Or in a country rich as this today.
Well, cloth was wanted that was white as snow,
But a sheep's fleece was seldom that, and so,
The cloth was stretched, and pounded with an earth
– yes, earth, in fact a special sort of clay –
That made it white.

When I say "pounded", what I mean is this.
Great wooden hammers, oak again of course,
Had to be lifted up and banged down hard
To drive the earth between the woollens' weave,
And the percussion had to be keen and quick
Beyond men's strength to do it hour by hour.
So I was needed, to provide the power,
'Cos, once my water flows, I never tire.
Ah, those were days for pride!

But those days passed,
And once again I hung above this stream,
Unmoving, 'till, one morning, months ago,
New engineers revived the mill above
With a new engine, which they called "turbine".
"Green electricity", they said,
Or some such name I'd never heard,
But, as before, they needed power.
"This wheel's still good", one said.
"Why waste its strength?"
And so, with two new paddles, and a gate
On the upstream sluice
           where worm had got the wood,
I'm back at work, and may I be again
For another thousand years, I say!

Free returns

Too short, too narrow, straps and bows
Gripping my insteps and my toes.
But I need new shoes for Tuesday
So I've brought them back; but look
At the queue!
                 Everyone's trying
"Wear once and return tomorrow.".
I can see the soup-stain on that
Skirt from here. The assistant must,
But, no, she doesn't care what state
It's in, or what the customer
Takes instead, so long as the price
Increases overall.
                 My turn.
Scuffed? Where? Good heavens, how did you
Find that? It must have been there when
I bought them. What do you mean, "No"?
What company policy? Well,
If that's your attitude, I think
I'll take the red ones, even if
They cost a little more. My card
Refused? …

To a carrot

O Carrot, fiery orange as you slide
Unwillingly but smoothly from the damp, dark earth,
Promising crispness in the fresh bite of sharp white teeth
Into your glistening, washed-clean body sacrificed
To an enthusiastic gardener's pangs, self-justified
By hours of care for the depth and friable fineness
Of the rich brown soil in which your seed was sown.

A gleaming sharp knife's edge awaits you in the kitchen
And boiling water, or the company
Of lettuce, red tomato, radish (formerly your neighbour)
In the rich central communal cut-glass bowl.

As season follows season, disguised, they still appear,
But wrapped in plastic, pre-washed, bought from shops,
And we will try to fool ourselves they're carrots,
Foreign carrots, but they won't be as you are.

Here's to those ...

Here's to those who picked me up
    When I tripped on the pavement edge
    An African man, a Chinese girl,
        The elderly lady who found my stick
        Beneath the car at the pavement edge
    From nowhere and everywhere
        Descending from the sky
    It seemed to me, flat on my back
            Along the pavement edge

Ode to my socks

(after Francisco X Alarcon)

I have
Ignored you for
Ten years

I had forgotten
The luxury
Of your warmth

The fun of
Your patterns
And colours

And left you
In the bottom drawer
Of the chest

Relegated
To my second bedroom
Where I never go

But when
I needed you
This morning

There you were
Ready
To offer comfort

On a
Freezing
January day

And I still couldn't
Reach my feet
To put you on

Three haikus: old bones
**(each of 17 syllables divided into
3 lines of 5, 7, and 5 syllables)**

Snow in November
More, more followed, locked me in
April sun brings life

Stagger just ten yards
Effort but great achievement
Company the prize

Aches bend my body
Does a gnarled ancient tree
Bend to ease its pain?

Index of titles

Index of first lines

Acknowledgements

"Two pools of blood", "Sulawesi tsunami, September 2018", "High on the mountain", "A wasted weekend", and "Silent sounds" were first published in "The Cannon's Mouth", the quarterly anthology of Cannon Poets.

Huge thanks are due to all the Cannon Poets for their warm welcome and invaluable advice, especially Di de Woolfson, Jenna Plews and Martin Underwood, and to the members of Solihull Writers' Workshop, to Lydia Towsey and the members of Word!, and to Charlie Jordan, for the inspiration repeatedly generated in their workshops.

All peculiarities of interpretation are my own.

RF
Summer, 2022

The author

Robert was a member of the University of
Cambridge Spitzbergen expedition, 1965 and
undertook research in Libya in 1966–67.
After graduation he lectured in environmental
sciences at the Universities of London and
Exeter before joining the UK Civil Service.
He later spent 7 years as a management
consultant, working with central and local
government organisations in the UK, Bulgaria
and Hungary and with major manufacturing
companies in Belgium, Germany, and the USA.
He began writing again after retiring. His earlier
poetry collection Late Starter was published in
2018. He has won prizes and commendations
in the Solihull Writer's Workshop annual poetry
and fiction competitions and has published
poems in the quarterly anthologies of the
Moseley-based Cannon Poets group. 11 of his
short stories are online at www.cafelit.co.uk.
His novel A Magic Flight was published in
September 2022.

Robert Ferguson

Start to Finish

ISBN 978-3-99131-754-8
74 pages

Wander through your life; the seasons, months, weather, national events, and personal pleasures. Sit with these poems, remember, and enjoy.